Measures

Peter Patilla

First published in Great Britain by Heinemann Library,
Halley Court, Jordan Hill, Oxford OX2 8EJ,
a division of Reed Educational and Professional Publishing Ltd.
Heinemann is a registered trademark of Reed Educational & Professional Publishing Limited.

OXFORD MELBOURNE AUCKLAND
JOHANNESBURG BLANTYRE GABORONE
IBADAN PORTSMOUTH NH (USA) CHICAGO

Designed by AMR
Illustrations by Jessica Stockham (Beehive Illustration)
Originated by HBM Print Ltd, Singapore
Printed and bound by South China Printing Co., Hong Kong/China

03 02 01 00 99
10 9 8 7 6 5 4 3 2 1

ISBN 0 431 09353 9

British Library Cataloguing in Publication Data
Patilla, Peter
 Measures. – (Maths links)
 I.Mensuration – Juvenile literature
 I.Title.
 516.1·5

Acknowledgements
The Publishers would like to thank the following for permission to reproduce photographs:
Trevor Clifford, pgs 4, 5, 7, 8, 9, 10, 11, 14, 15, 16, 17, 18, 19, 20, 21, 22, 23, 25, 27, 28, 29.

Cover photograph reproduced with permission of Trevor Clifford.

Our thanks to David Kirkby for his comments in the preparation of this book.

Every effort has been made to contact copyright holders of any material reproduced in this book. Any omissions will be rectified in subsequent printings if notice is given to the Publisher.

For more information about Heinemann Library books, or to order, please phone +44 (0)1865 888066, or send a fax to +44 (0)1865 314091. You can visit our website at www.heinemann.co.uk

Contents

Some words are shown in bold, **like this**. You can find out what they mean by looking in the Glossary.

Is it the right size?

much too large

much too small

just the right size

Sometimes things are too big. Sometimes they are too small. We like things to be just the right size.

4

Tops should fit onto bottoms, otherwise the
things inside would fall out.

Can you find which tops go with which bottoms?

Smallest and largest

largest

smallest

same size

When things are close together, it is easy to see which are about the same size. You can also see which is largest and which is smallest.

6

Here is a jumble of different objects. Some are sets which go together.

Which is the largest and which is the smallest you can see in each set? Which is medium-sized?

Opposites

tall
ladder

little
brush

short
ladder

big
brush

When we talk about sizes, we often use words
which describe opposites, such as big and little, or
tall and short.

There are lots of opposite sizes in the picture. Deep and shallow, wide and narrow, large and small, thick and thin, and long and short: these are all opposite words.

Which opposite words best fit the pairs of objects in the picture?

Comparing lengths

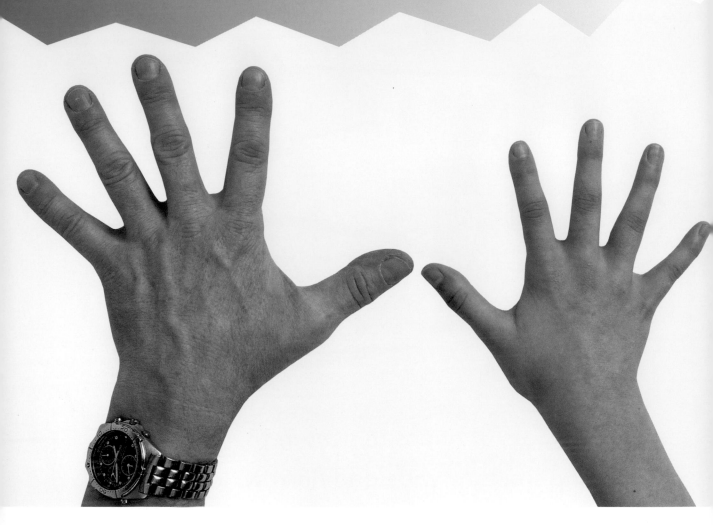

Many, many years ago people measured things using parts of their body, such as their hand. This was a problem. The measurements were not always the same.

These objects are being measured with **standard units**. The units used are all the same size.

What is being used as the standard unit?
How many units does each object measure?

11

Measuring lengths

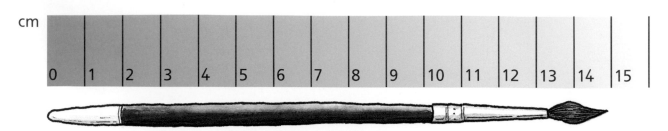

This paintbrush measures 15 cm.

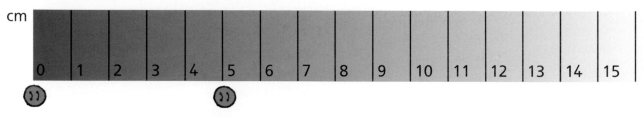

The distance between these buttons is 5 cm.

cm is a short way of writing centimetre.
m is a short way of writing metre.

We use rulers or tapes to measure short lengths
and distances in **centimetres**. Longer lengths are
measured in **metres**. One metre is as long as
100 centimetres.

cm

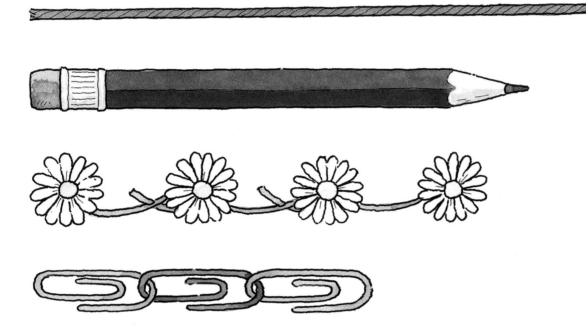

An **estimate** is a sensible guess. Estimate each of these lengths in centimetres. Use a ruler to check your estimates.

Estimate and check some more lengths in centimetres. Are you good at estimating lengths?

13

Comparing weight

same weight

heavier  lighter

Sometimes we can tell whether things are heavier, lighter, or about the same by picking them up. Other times we need to use a **balance** to find out. The heavier side of a balance goes down.

14

Look at the bunches of bananas.

Which of the bunches of bananas do you think will be the heaviest? Which will be the lightest? Which will be about the same weight?

Measuring weight

We can measure weight using gram and kilogram weights.

We can read the weight on the dial.

We use a **balance** and **weights** to find out how heavy something is. Each weight has a number of **grams** or **kilograms** written on it. We can also use **scales** and read the weight from the dial.

Things which are quite light are weighed in grams. Heavier things are weighed in kilograms.

Look at the objects and say what you think each one would be weighed in.

Comparing capacity

nearly full

nearly empty

half full

empty

full

Capacity is how much something will hold. Things can be full, empty or somewhere in between. We can use liquid or dry things to find the capacity of containers.

Look at the glasses and jugs on this party table.

Which is the full glass? Which is the empty glass? Which glass is about half full?

Measuring capacity

All these containers have the same amount inside them.

We use **litres,** half litres and **millilitres** to find out how much something holds. A litre can look very different when the containers are different shapes.

Each of these containers has a different **capacity**.

Estimate which holds more than a litre. Which do you think hold less than a litre? Do any hold about a litre?

21

Comparing volumes

Heavy things do not always take up a lot of space. Light things sometimes take up a lot of space. The amount of space something takes up is its **volume**.

When packing things away, we must think about how much space we will need. We have to think whether everything will fit into the space we have.

Which pile of clothes will fit easily into the case?

Comparing temperatures

Some of these things are very hot and some are cold.

Temperature is about how hot, cold or warm something is. We sometimes say the temperature is boiling or freezing.

24

When the temperature is cold, we want to keep warm. When it is hot, we want to keep cool.

Which clothes would help keep us warm?
Which clothes would help keep us cool?

Measuring temperature

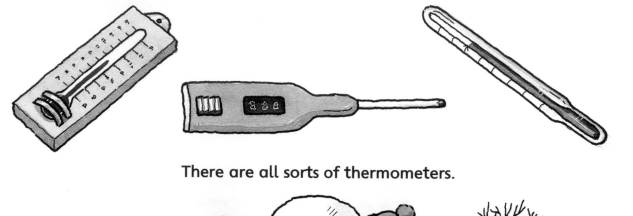

There are all sorts of thermometers.

Sometimes it snows when the temperature is very cold.

Thermometers are used to measure temperature. They measure it in **degrees**. They show us if a person or place is hot or cold.

Sometimes we need to raise the temperature of food by cooking it. Sometimes we cool or freeze foods, so they will keep longer.

Look at the picture. What is best eaten hot? What is best eaten cold?

Comparing sizes

Drawings and models can be larger, smaller or the same size as the real thing.

Toy models may be smaller, larger or the same size as the real thing.

Which of these toys are about the same size as the real thing? Which are smaller than the real thing?

Glossary

balance simple machine used to compare the weight of two things

capacity how much something will hold

centimetre small standard unit used in length. This page is about 20 cm wide.

degree standard unit used to measure temperature

estimate a good guess

gram small standard unit used in weight

kilogram standard unit used in weight. Weighs 1000 grams.

litre a large standard unit used in capacity. It is about 4 large cupfuls of water.

metre standard unit used in length. The length of 100 centimetres.

millilitre small standard unit used in capacity. A teaspoon holds about 5 millilitres.

scales machine that weighs how heavy something is. It has dials.

standard units measuring units which are all the same size. Identical paperclips can be used as standard units.

temperature how hot or cold something is

thermometers measure how hot something is in units called degrees. (Boiling water is very hot, a frozen ice cube is very cold.)

volume how much space or room something takes up

weights gram and kilogram weights are used to find how heavy something is

Fact file

Length: kilometres (km), metres (m), centimetres (cm), millimetres (mm)

10 mm = 1 cm
100 cm = 1 m
1000 m = 1 km

Weight: kilograms (kg), grams (g), milligrams (mg)

1000 mg = 1 g
1000 g = 1 kg
1000 kg = 1 t

Capacity: litres (l), millilitres (ml)

1000 ml = 1 l

Temperature: degrees (°) Centigrade/Celsius (C)

0°C = freezing water
100°C = boiling water

Answers

page 9	deep and shallow boxes; long and short flowers; large and small bricks; wide and narrow ribbon; thick and thin string
page 11	plant and pot = 9 paperclips tall, glass = 8 paperclips around, pencil = 6 paperclips long
page 15	heaviest = 5 banana bunch, lightest = 2 banana bunch, same = 4 banana bunches
page 17	bricks and oranges = kilograms, cotton wool balls and feathers = grams
page 21	bucket and large bowl hold more than one litre; shallow dish and saucepan hold about a litre; bottle, jug, mug, ladle and small bowl all hold less than a litre
page 23	3.

Index